SEVEN DAYS OF GOD'S PROCESS

Russell E. Walden

ISBN: 1545431795
ISBN 13: 9781545431795

INTRODUCTION

<u>In the Beginning:</u>

Throughout the word of God, we find reference to the "Day of the Lord". God works in a timeframe of days. When he readied Noah to go into the ark, He chose a specific number of days prior, to notify him:

> *[Gen 7:4 KJV] 4 For yet seven days, and I will cause it to rain upon the earth forty days and forty nights; and every living substance that I have made will I destroy from off the face of the earth.*

You can ask the Father "how long" and the answer is always the same. Seven days. This is more than a chronological span of time. Seven speaks of perfection. It is about God's Kairos timing moving into Chronos reality or manifestation. Seven days. Is this some random number of days that just so happened to be the time that God tells Noah that the rains were coming? Looking back at creation in Gen. 1:1 to Gen. 2:3, we find that God chose seven days in which to create the earth. God being God, we know that He could have simply made all things in the blink of an eye, including man, but He did not. He took seven specific time frames in which He acted in an exact manner and in an order that has meaning for us, if we will take time to study it.

The Significance of the Number Seven:

The term "seven days" appears 92 times in the scriptures, compassing both the Old and the New testaments. The majority of these references are contained in the law of Moses, giving specific requirements regarding the statutes and commandments. God apparently intended to impress upon the ancient Hebrews the importance and weight He places on the number seven. What does this mean to us? Paul taught that the Old Testament comprises for us a shadow that point to the substance of New Testament reality you and I can discern about spiritual things, and how to cooperate with the mandates of the kingdom in our lives:

> *[1Co 10:11 KJV] 11 Now all these things happened unto them for ensamples: and they are written for our admonition, upon whom the ends of the world are come.*

If the concept of seven days is so prominently displayed in the scriptures, then God is telling us something we need to pay attention to. What can we learn from the number seven itself? Again, the number seven is a number that is generally believed to have a spiritual meaning connected with perfection. The number seven appears 735 times in the bible, 54 times alone in the book of Revelation. There are Hebrew traditions that maintain that Adam was created on the seventh month on the seventh day, 5777 years ago. The word "created" is used seven times in the creation account of Gen. 1:1 – 2:4 (specifically Genesis 1:1, 21, 27 three times; 2:3; 2:4). The number seven, therefore, is not only connected with perfection, but also with creation or "to create". Creation is both cosmic and universal, as well as personal and intimate to our lives. God is still creating. Everything God does in our life is creative in nature. If the number seven and creation ARE linked, then we would be benefited by discovering this linkage and posturing ourselves, in faith and action, to the process revealed thereby.

The Hebrew word for "seventh" or "seven" means "vow or oath" or "to cut". In employing this number in connection with creation, God was foreshadowing His own foreknowledge that man would fall, and a separation would be the result that would then be ameliorated by the covenantal "cutting" or outpouring of the life of Jesus upon the cross. In looking at the number seven, we are not attempting to install in your life some convoluted mystical process by which you can leverage God to move in your behalf. In looking at God's process, we are seeking to understand how, in our commitment to Christ, we might position ourselves directly in front of the cross of Christ. We want to press ourselves out of a human experience of performance and humanism, into the reality and fullness of all that Jesus has paid for in our stead. The claims of Christ applied to your life are not instantaneous. They are conditional and provisional. They involve process and initiation on God's part, and humility and cooperation on your part. God has already done what He is going to do in Christ. Now the door stands open to us to step in, by cooperative acts of humility and yieldedness, to see the miraculous become the norm and not the exception in our lives.

[Mat 5:33 KJV] 33 Again, ye have heard that it hath been said by them of old time, Thou shalt not forswear thyself, but shalt perform unto the Lord thine oaths:

Again, the number seven relates to covenant, cutting and the idea of vows or oaths. When the scripture says that we should perform our vows or oaths unto the Lord, it is literally taken that unto the Lord we should perform our "sevens". Being that seven relates to the living out of our days then, from God's perspective, your days are your oath before Him (just as we believe, on a human level, that a man's word is his bond). In other words, Jesus is saying in Matt. 5:33, that you should not take an oath, for YOUR LIFE is an oath lived out before God, as far as God originally intended and is concerned. To take an oath beyond this is to cheapen your own life and give yourself an opportunity or option, to reflect something other than God's innate character in your person.

Jesus is saying that an oath is not something you merely take as an occasional protestation of your veracity or intention. An oath is something you live out. Your life is an oath to God and every breath a vow. Your life is intended by God to be as solemn as the most dread vow you could ever take. The days of our lives lived out before the Lord, are in some sense, as sacramental in the eyes of God as the most solemn oath that one might take.

The Glyph for Number Seven:
The glyph for the number seven is called by many linguists and ancient numerologists a "crowned vav", or a crowned number six. This is because the glyph or symbol for the number six is identical to the number seven with the addition of a thrice-spired crown added to the top (denoting Father, Son and Holy Ghost?). Six is the number of man and often used as the word "and" in the Hebrew portion of the Old Testament (for instance: "in the beginning God created the heavens AND [vav] the earth). The number six represents the number of man. When Jesus called Himself the "son of man", He was in effect calling Himself "the son of six". The "vav" or number six, is also the central consonant of the Torah (first 5 books of the bible). The Pharisees and scholars of Jesus' day would have been very aware of this. In John 5:39, Jesus told the Pharisees that the scriptures they loved testified of Him. In other words, when they looked

in the scriptures, they saw the "vav" or "son of man" at the very center of their beloved Torah.

The number seven is the son of man (6) crowned and perfected (7). This uniquely applies to Jesus but also applies to us, because of the dual meaning in the number seven of covenant or cutting. Covenant implies two parties involved. Jesus cut the covenant, not only to establish that He is the crowned King of heaven, but also to establish the authority of the believer. In Luke 13:32, when Jesus told Herod that on the third day He would be perfected, this is also a reference to the number seven, which means or represents perfection, specifically spiritual perfection or perfection in the kingdom. It would not do violence to the meaning to think of Jesus as saying "on the third day I will be sevened [or, crowned]".

> *[Luk 13:32 KJV] ... to day and to morrow, and the third [day] I shall be perfected.*

Notice, Jesus was not saying that He was perfect, but that He was being perfected. In other words, He was identifying Himself in connection to God's process.

> *[Luk 2:40 KJV] 40 And the child grew, and waxed strong in spirit, filled with wisdom: and the grace of God was upon him.*

Whatever you think about Jesus as being perfect, these verses tell us that we are being perfected. That implies process. The meaning of the number seven connects it with God's process. There were seven stages or days of Jesus' life.

1. His birth
2. His Childhood
3. His adolescence

4. Year of Obscurity
5. Year of Popularity
6. Year of Opposition
7. Death, Burial and Resurrection

When Jesus tells Herod "today and tomorrow I do miracles and the third day I will be perfected", He was in the year (or, day) of popularity of His public ministry. He was saying, He would fulfill that day and the next and then be perfected through death, burial and resurrection. The reality that Jesus was IN PROCESS explains to us His prayer life:

> *[Heb 5:7 KJV] 7 Who in the days of his flesh, when he had offered up prayers and supplications with strong crying and tears unto him that was able to save him from death, and was heard in that he feared;*

Why was Jesus so stressed out? Why was He crying and in tears? Was He afraid of the devil? Not likely. He knew He was in process. He had a cup to drink. The cup is God's process. He endured the cross for the joy that was set before Him, but He knew, and we should all know, that there is PROCESS that precedes OUTCOME in God. You cannot have the throne without the cross. You cannot have the fruit without the seed falling into the ground and dying. Again, Pentecost and the Charismatic movement have focused too much on spontaneous outcome. They have drilled down on this to the point that some think this is the ONLY WAY to receive from God. They don't understand that yes, there can be instantaneous deliverance and answers, but of all the things God can and will bring into your life spontaneously, like a dollop of Holy Ghost whip cream on your head – you can likewise WALK INTO, by God's process. In fact, God's process is the one constant in our lives that, if we COOPERATE, we will come inexorably to outcome, as Jesus Himself did in the death, burial and resurrection.

The Working of Miracles:

Looking at the number seven in this way then, we see it relates to the idea of kingdom authority conferred by the covenantal transaction of the cross, conferred upon men through the Lord Jesus Christ, the crowned son of man. This was not an instantaneous act or declaration. There were steps involved and process employed over time. The laying out of seven days and the events contained in them speak to us of process. Authority is not the mere waving of a scepter. Again, God could have done this and made an instantaneous creation, but He did not. Likewise, in redemption, He could have simply declared over humanity 2000 years ago, "I redeem you", but He did not. God is a God of process. The Pentecostal / Charismatic obsession with instantaneously receiving from God, as the only valid or authentic means of the Father's intervention, robs them of the miracle that involves, and in fact demands, process.

> *[Gal 3:5 KJV] 5 He therefore that ministereth to you the Spirit, and worketh miracles among you, [doeth he it] by the works of the law, or by the hearing of faith?*

Miracles are part of the nine gifts of the Spirit listed in 1 Cor. 12:8-10. Miracles are different from the other 8 gifts, because according to the apostle Paul in Gal. 3:5, miracles must be worked. They seldom function like some dollop of Holy Ghost whip cream being doused upon the top of your head. They very often involve process and action, including cooperation on the part of the person receiving the miracle. Even in the life and ministry of Jesus, He at times performed instantaneous miracles, but often, apparently chose to resort to an applied process, in order to effect miraculous recovery of various cases.

In one place, Jesus made clay of his saliva and put it on a man's eyes to heal blindness:

> *[Jhn 9:6 KJV] 6 When he had thus spoken, he spat on the ground, and made clay of the spittle, and he anointed the eyes of the blind man with the clay,*

In another instance, Jesus took a man aside from the crowd and spit on him to recover the person from a deaf and dumb state:

> *[Mar 7:33 KJV] 33 And he took him aside from the multitude, and put his fingers into his ears, and he spit, and touched his tongue;*

In still another situation, Jesus took a man for a walk, specifically out of town, in order to effect healing from blindness:

> *[Mar 8:23-25 KJV] 23 And he took the blind man by the hand, and led him out of the town; and when he had spit on his eyes, and put his hands upon him, he asked him if he saw ought. 24 And he looked up, and said, I see men as trees, walking. 25 After that he put [his] hands again upon his eyes, and made him look up: and he was restored, and saw every man clearly.*

Why would Jesus do things this way? Is He simply mixing it up because He is bored and wants to try something new? We know, if we accept Him for who He is, that He could have simply, with a word, healed every person in the earth in a moment of time, but He didn't. He chose in His earth walk (and God Himself chose in creation) to act in the context of process. God is a God of process and that requires initiative on our part, not only to hear, but to act in expectation of an outcome when we follow the leading of the

Holy Spirit in our lives. We may be called upon to do many unusual things, but if they are led by God, they will have an outcome.

Is God's process learnable or totally random? The Genesis account helps us, if we choose to dig deeper into the narrative of Genesis 1 and 2. In it, we see God moving upon the chaos of whatever existed before He made the heavens and the earth. He doesn't, in this case, move spontaneously or instantaneously. He moves deliberately and within a regimented number of days in a specific order. He could have made man first and light last. He could have made dry land and then seas. God is God and He can do anything He wants anytime He wants, therefore, in examining the order in which He DID act, we can only conclude there was a reason for doing so that was not of necessity, but in fact, leaving clues and examples for us who would examine these accounts later, so we could understand something of His process and cooperate with it in our own lives. Process brings outcome. God's process functions according to learnable truths, that represent a framework of authenticity, within which, we can anticipate and even provoke what happens next as we move in the things of God from a posture of want, need and necessity, to a place of total outcome and destiny.

CHAPTER 1
DAY ONE

Introduction:
In the first chapter, we examined the significance of the day of the Lord in conjunction with the number seven and its particular meaning. God is a God of process. He is not bound by any particular means by which He must act. Therefore, His chosen methods are not of necessity, but rather are saying something to us of His arbitrary and independent character. God created in seven days, instead of one instantaneous moment, because He wants us to understand something of His process. He wants us, as dear children, to emulate in our environment what He demonstrated in His when He saw the chaos of the deep. What are you doing with the chaos that you see in your life?

Likewise, in the New Covenant, Jesus says in Luke 17, that the kingdom of God is not something we are mere observers to, but in fact, He intends that we cooperate with Him in His anointed process, by which He brings His graces and gifts to bear in our lives for the purpose of benefit, dividend and breakthrough.

[Luk 17:20-21 KJV] 20 And when he was demanded of the Pharisees, when the kingdom of God should come, he answered them and said, The kingdom of God cometh not with observation: 21 Neither shall they say, Lo here! or, lo there! for, behold, the kingdom of God is within you.

We can see from this scripture above that whatever the kingdom is – the understanding Jesus wants us to have is more about something taking its impetus within our own hearts and lives than something that can be charted on an eschatological graph. The kingdom is not something we interact with from an independent point of observation. You cannot accurately perceive ANYTHING about the kingdom from a measurement drawn from objective observation. It is something living and vital within us spilling out in our lives through a collaborative process that demands our cooperation. Faith without works is dead because the inherent nature of the kingdom is so intrinsically collaborative that one of the primary names of God is Paraclete meaning, "one brought alongside together against". God will do nothing without securing man's partnership and collaboration in His anointed process. In the absence of collaboration and cooperation, the only result is to find yourself excluded from everything the kingdom is and the benefit intended to be your portion.

God's Sense of Timing:

In revealing His process over and over in scripture, we are given to understand that God works in the framework of particular days. A day, as God would have us understand it, cannot be construed to merely refer to a 24-hour period, or a series of days making up weeks, months or years. Peter, in speaking of this, broadens our understanding of God's timing as being much more broad and flexible than we might think in our own finite perspective. God desires for us to be an integral part of His process, for He is not willing to do what He is going to do in the earth without your cooperation.

On the First Day:

[Gen 1:1-31 KJV] 1 In the beginning God created the heaven and the earth. 2 And the earth was without form, and void; and darkness [was] upon the face of the deep. And the Spirit of God moved upon the face of the waters.

Each day of creation reveals something distinct about God's character. Each day of creation reveals something unique, that is then extended or repeated throughout the span of what follows. What is the significance for us of this first day of creation, other than as a point of sacred history telling us where the natural world came from? As God acted at the macro-level to create the earth, so He acts at the micro-level in equal measure and means in your individual life and situation. Understanding this gives insight into the beginning, middle and end of what God is doing in your situation, regardless of the variables. In this way, you can provide the necessary collaboration that we have already shown is essential in terms of seeing what the kingdom IS, to then become what you EXPERIENCE in whatever challenge you may be facing at the time.

When I was reading Gen. 7:4, I heard the question "God, when are you going to act in my situation?" The answer came by what I read in the verse "for yet seven days..." Have you ever asked God when He was going to move in your circumstances? The answer is always the same! Gen. 7:4 tells us: "in seven days..." This is far more than seven 24-hour time frames, and then your answer miraculously appears. The day of the Lord, as a concept in scripture, implies purpose, sovereignty and Lordship on God's part, and cooperation, humility and repentance on man's part. This series of teachings is all about answering that one cosmic question in your life:

What time is it?

The answer is different for everyone. This is God's Kairos timing. The fullness of time in your life will come at a different time than the fullness of God in my life. The common need for both you and I is to know WHAT DAY IT IS, and what does that day require of us in terms of cooperation and yielding? Waiting on God can be a frustrating thing. This was the problem the laborers had in the parable Jesus gave of the householder in Matt. 20:1-16. Some were paid the same for working all day, as others were paid for working just an hour. The conclusion of this parable is in verse 16, "many are called – but few are chosen". It is all about NOT getting offended, because GOD'S TIMING in one person's life is different from His timing in yours. Jesus said 4 times in scripture, "behold I come quickly" and it has been 2000 years. How are we to interpret this? What is expected of us in the light of the fact that God's reckoning of time and man's reckoning of time are two different things?

The First Day:

> *[Gen 1:1-2 KJV] 1 In the beginning God created the heaven and the earth. 2 And the earth was without form, and void; and darkness [was] upon the face of the deep. And the Spirit of God moved upon the face of the waters. 3 And God said, Let there be light: and there was light. 4 And God saw the light, that [it was] good: and God divided the light from the darkness. 5 And God called the light Day, and the darkness he called Night. And the evening and the morning were the first day.*

> *When the scriptures say, in the beginning God created the heavens and the earth, the word create there includes the meaning that implies, He "carved out" the heavens and the earth. What did He carve the heavens and the earth out of? Out of the deep. Out of a field*

of potential before Him that was initially without form and void. Quantum theorists surmise that the 3 dimensional universe sprang into existence in what they call a "big bang". They understand that this coming into existence had to originate from somewhere. What Genesis calls "the deep", scientists call the field of all possibilities. It has been proven that at a quantum level, this field responds, in a creative way, to being observed. This is called the Copenhagen effect, that says a quantum particle exists in all places at once until it is observed, and then it blinks into existence. Once observed, it transforms, by virtue of an existing observation, from a probability wave to an existent particle. Further, to the chagrin of these logical minds, they have determined that not only does the wave become a particle once observed, but that it actually will then behave in a manner that the observer anticipates and expects it to behave.

The Spirit of God Moved on the Face of the Deep:
On the first day, God moved or brooded over the deep or the void – that which had yet to reflect His purpose and potential. The original word here means that God brooded over the deep as a hen broods over its young. The word also means "to cherish young" as an eagle cherishes its chicks. In other words, this was not a dispassionate act. God was then, as He is now – the personification of love according to 1 John 4:8 - and in love He was acting. Many people try to "faith" things into existence that are born, not of love, but of selfishness. Napoleon Hill in his classic "Think and Grow Rich", taught that it was not enough to simply believe and declare that you will be wealthy – for that is a selfish goal. He taught rather that a declaration made, only became creative when it was born of altruistic passion to serve others, and then the belief took on a dynamism that would transform any life.

[Pro 4:23 KJV] 23 Keep thy heart with all diligence; for out of it [are] the issues of life.

Where did life and creation originate? In the heart of God. All of creation issued forth out of the Spirit of God that was hovering, creatively, over the deep, and from that, took the outward circumstance and conformed it to His inward reality, and the earth was brought forth in all of its potentiality. You likewise are made in God's image. Your outward circumstance originates and is sustained and maintained according to Proverbs 4:23, within your own inner man. Like it or not, if you are enduring what is not to your taste in life, the answer originates, not in some cosmic twist of fate that has denied you what you long for, but actually from within your person, your own inner man. That contaminated issue came forth, empowered with the tenterhooks of your own passions, to lay hold on what was outwardly, and form and fashion it from its potential state, into a state reflecting what is in your own heart. In other words, if you don't like what is in your life, then change what is in your heart. Your heart – what is in your heart in abundance, will get out of your mouth and into the earth and WILL inexorably shape and control your environment. This is not a mere possibility, it is an inviolate manifestation that establishes the fact that you are made in the image of God, and as He created that which He desired from within Himself, so what you are experiencing originated from within your own person. Therein lies both the dilemma of man and the path of progress, if you will choose to learn the avenue by which you exit from the confinement of sinful man's thoughts and the world they create, and adopt the mind of the Spirit and the limitless life of potential it will create – all from within your own heart and spirit, you will walk out the plan of God for your life.

In verse 2, God said "let there be light" and there was light. How could God create light? Because He WAS and still is LIGHT:

[1Jo 1:5 KJV] 5 This then is the message which we have heard of him, and declare unto you, that God is light, and in him is no darkness at all.

In other words, when God spoke His words, He arrested the deep and conformed it to who and what He was. Likewise, in Matt. 5:14, Jesus said, you are the light of the world. In this sense, Jesus is leading us to believe that at some existential level, we ARE what God is. He took the outward circumstances and not only conformed it by His words to what was IN Him – He took WHO He was and compelled, by the power of His word. The deep responded and was formed and fashioned into that which reflected His character. This is what is in Him, establishing the heavens and the earth, and this is what is IN YOU, establishing your spiritual, relational and material environment. If you don't like what you see, the path of change comes by dealing with YOURSELF and what is in you, before addressing the outward. If you can't discern yourself, then you will never appropriately or accurately discern your situation fully enough to have any hope of change.

We see then that on the first day, God most significantly did the following:

1. Moved upon the face of the deep.
2. He spoke and conformed the deep – an outward environment, compelling it by His words to conform, to come to parity to the inward atmosphere of who He was. Out of His heart came the issues of life and the cosmos was created.

Likewise, you are to emulate God, according to Eph. 5:1, doing in your life what He did in the recorded past.

1. Moving on the face of your deep – the outward circumstances.
2. Speaking and conforming the deep – your outward environment, compelling it, by your faith filled words, to come to parity to the inward atmosphere of who you are in Christ inwardly. This is what Jesus meant when He said "on earth

7

as it is in heaven. In your outward circumstance, as it is in heaven (your inward reality in Christ – the kingdom is in you).

If you are looking out on your life and all you see is unrealized potential, then you are in day one of God's process and this is your prerogative. To do what He would do, were He in your position. We know what He would do, for we have a record of what He did do. He moved out, by His Spirit, over that deep – that unrealized potential and fully discerned it, fixed His determination upon it and compelled it to come to parity with the inward reality of who He was at that moment. Go and do thou likewise!

CHAPTER 2
DAY TWO

Containment, Division and Calling:

I n the first day, God brooded or moved over the face of the deep and created light. Darkness was not something that was created, it was part of the void that was dispelled by light. Now realize that the sun and stars have not been created, so light is existing without a source of light. God is a God who never does anything in a row. There is very little true symmetry that is naturally occurring, so if you expect God to operate in the context of your understanding, then you are limiting God.

> *[Psa 78:41 KJV] 41 Yea, they turned back and tempted God, and limited the Holy One of Israel.*

How do we limit God? When we require Him to conduct Himself in a fashion that makes sense to us. Many times, people cry and weep saying "if I just understood what God was doing in my life, I would get on board and cooperate..." Let me say this to you: understanding is highly overrated. Consider the words of Isaiah concerning guidance of the Holy Spirit in your life:

[Isa 55:12 KJV] 12 For ye shall go out with joy, and be led forth with peace: the mountains and the hills shall break forth before you into singing, and all the trees of the field shall clap [their] hands.

It doesn't say you will go out with understanding and be led with intellect. You go out with joy and are led forth with peace. If you want to move at the speed of Godspeed acceleration in the Spirit, you must get in the fast lane of peace and joy and be willing to leave understanding behind:

[Phl 4:7 KJV] 7 And the peace of God, which passeth all understanding, shall keep your hearts and minds through Christ Jesus.

Many people say "well, God will never do anything contrary to His word..." and that is true. This is a true statement, but what this person is really saying is that God will never do anything contrary to THEIR UNDERSTANDING of the WORD, and that is absolutely untrue. God will often and with abandon, act in your life and compel you to cooperate with Him in ways that you will not initially understand, although if you ask Him, He will explain, but only AFTER you have obeyed.

In other words, if you want what you have never had before, you must be willing to go where you have never been before. If you are going to go in God where you have never been before, you are going to have to be willing to think about God and the things of God in ways you have never thought in times past. You see, things are the way they are because of what you are doing. If you want what you have never had before, you must be willing to do what you have never done before. This is not just a call to random chaos. It is a call to come out of your mind, into the mind of Christ and be willing, in yourself, not to demand that God explain Himself to you as a condition of obedience. Dangerous? You bet! No guts – no glory. Any radical opportunity for breakthrough and benefit in the things of God also opens you up to catastrophic failure – this is what the life of faith is - RISK TAKING. Not the calculated risk of a natural perspective, but the inspired risk, based on the leading of the Holy Spirit, that compels you to check your rationale at the door and be willing to be a water walker in God!

You might insist, "I've taken risks before and it didn't work out". My response would be, where were your passions placed? Were you pursuing something for yourself or were you moving in love? Love never fails. If you failed, then let the scripture discern what happened. That may sting a little, but do you want to nurse the wounds of past failure – or get up, dust yourself off and walk into the glory of your next success by the leading of the Holy Spirit. Quit feeling sorry for yourself and move on!

The Firmament of the Heavens:
In the first day then, we see that God moves, broods and speaks. He brings forth, out of Himself, that which He wishes to surround Himself with. He does so with words. He is willing and desiring to have what is IN HIM to become the environment which is around Him. Ask yourself the question – do you want what is IN YOU to be what is AROUND you, ordering your life and controlling what happens next? Ever since God created light, He has acted every single day, taking OBLIGATORY responsibility for that which He has created. If you are ever going to participate in God's process, the first responsibility is to get your INWARD ENVIRONMENT (the kingdom is within you) in line with God's character, heart and spirit – otherwise, out of your heart will come the issues of a life that will defeat you, break your heart and torpedo your destiny.

The Second Day: Containment:

6 And God said, Let there be a firmament in the midst of the waters, and let it divide the waters from the waters. 7 And God made the firmament, and divided the waters which [were] under the firmament from the waters which [were] above the firmament: and it was so. 8 And God called the firmament Heaven. And the evening and the morning were the second day.

In the second day, God made that which could not be contained in the FIRST day to be contained in the second day. In the first day, there was light and in the second day a firmament to set a boundary for light. It is the analogy of a wine skin. Every vintage of what God is doing in your life must come to containment in order to be preserved and propagated beyond its initial glory.

[Mar 2:22 KJV] 22 And no man putteth new wine into old bottles: else the new wine doth burst the bottles, and the wine is spilled, and the bottles will be marred: but new wine must be put into new bottles.

Many people hesitate right here. They don't want what one writer called the "harness of the Lord". In the writing by Bill Britton, there were two colts in the meadow. They loved their freedom, kicking up their heels and enjoying the sunshine. Then one day the Master came and introduced them to the harness. One colt rebelled, jumped fence and fled. The other submitted, and because the remaining colt submitted, he was allowed to step into his destiny of pulling the King's Carriage!

Are You Willing?
Are you willing to live the life of divine constraint and boundaries set by the Father, and not by you or others? Are you willing to look at the liberty that others have and hear the Father say clearly

to you, "others may, but you cannot"? You see – God made light and then created a firmament for light to be contained in – a jurisdiction if you will, for it to be manifest and operate within. Paul absolutely understood this. He knew that he had a certain spiritual firmament and jurisdiction within which to operate, and if he stepped out of that jurisdiction, he was powerless and in trouble. Have you ever felt powerless and in trouble?

[1Co 9:2 KJV] 2 If I be not an apostle unto others, yet doubtless I am to you: for the seal of mine apostleship are ye in the Lord.

[2Co 10:13-14 KJV] 13 But we will not boast of things without [our] measure, but according to the measure of the rule which God hath distributed to us, a measure to reach even unto you. 14 For we stretch not ourselves beyond [our measure], as though we reached not unto you: for we are come as far as to you also in [preaching] the gospel of Christ:

The firmament of the heavens was the measure of the environment within, which light was to manifest and operate according to God's purpose. You are light in the Lord, and in God according to the pattern, you have a firmament or jurisdiction in which to fulfill your purpose to be that light to everything and everyone within that boundary and parameter. Jesus warned us not to put our light under a bushel – in other words, not setting for ourselves an arbitrary boundary by telling God what you will and won't do.

[Mat 5:15 KJV] 15 Neither do men light a candle, and put it under a bushel, but on a candlestick; and it giveth light unto all that are in the house.

Rather, we are to say, as Jesus did at Gethsemane – "not my will but thine be done". Then you can fully populate the jurisdiction and measure that God has given you authority over. In this yieldedness, Jesus found the ultimate reward at the right hand of God. We are told then that we are seated with Christ in heavenly places. You might complain, "well it doesn't feel like it" – but only because you must first go to your Gethsemane, where you relinquish your boundaries for HIS, and allow God to take you further than your self-interest will allow you to go in fulfilling HIS purposes in your life (with your time, energy, resources and money) and not your independent ideas based on a darkened understanding.

God Divided in the Second Day:

In the second day, we see that God took that which was uncontained and created containment. Up to that time, nothing had been contained before, EVER. Likewise, in the second day, God divided the waters above the firmament from the waters that were under the firmament. In other words, God introduced division. Nothing had ever been divided before. When you look at what He actually did, He surrounded or encapsulated the visible creation with a canopy of water covering an inward body of water. Water above and water beneath. This was the earth as God originally intended it. What was the water above? What God caused to come down when He brought the flood. Not only did the flood come, but there was a visible corona of water orbiting the earth that many believed contributed to the longevity of man by shielding him from the harmful rays of the cosmos. Either way, the point is, that taking the macro-perspective and looking at our own lives - water represents SPIRIT. God wants us to experience a DIVISION in our beings and our lives by which the SPIRIT ABOVE is over-arching all that is taking place, and the SPIRIT beneath is coming up as the mist of God's favor, causing all to be fruitful and full of life.

Most people are unwilling to accept division. We preach against it. If division comes, we think that is a bad thing. We have a Babel mentality – we want everyone to speak the same language. Jesus said He didn't come to bring every one together, but to bring a sword.

> *[Mat 10:34 KJV] 34 Think not that I am come to send peace on earth: I came not to send peace, but a sword.*

Face the fact that in your life there are times that you are going to obey God, when momma and daddy might not like it. It may be a deal breaker for them. That doesn't mean that you are necessarily out of God's will. It may mean that you are walking out the second day of the creative process God is bringing about in your life, where your dependency is fully upon Him and not any other resource.

Calling:

> *[Gen 1:8 KJV] 8 And God called the firmament Heaven. And the evening and the morning were the second day.*

Finally, in the second day, we see something else that God does. He calls. Many are called but few are chosen. Why? Because they cannot endure the day of the Lord. There are seven days in God's process and many people, most people never get off second base. They cannot endure division. They think if everyone isn't getting along, then they need to turn back and do something else. They think if momma doesn't approve or the pastor doesn't approve, then somehow they must have missed God. Not necessarily. Likewise, those who miss their calling don't like to be contained. They want to have it all. Matthew 6:33 does promise this – but it is on God's terms and not ours.

> *[Mat 6:33 KJV] 33 But seek ye first the kingdom of God, and his righteousness; and all these things shall be added unto you.*

Most fail right here. They want what they want and they want it on their terms. Oh, they don't put it that way. They complain as victims, as sweet rebels – "I just don't understand…" and they turn away from the high calling with heavy hearts, full of self-pity, because God has refused to bow to the tyranny of their intellect, demanding that He act in a manner that makes sense to them.

If you are going to have the "and God called" moment over your life, you must be willing to accept separation, containment and division. You must be willing to accept containment and constraint upon you that is not imposed upon others. You must be willing to cooperate with the process of God's seven days that may not always make sense to you, because God wants to get you out of the sense realm and the mental realm, into the realm of His mind and His limitlessness.

CHAPTER 3
DAY THREE

Arriving at Seed Time and Harvest:

First Day: God Moved by His Spirit on the Deep
                 He Spoke and Created
Second Day: He Established Boundaries for His Creation
                 He Brought Division between things above
                 and things Beneath
                 He Called and Declared a Fixed Vision of
                 What He Created
Third Day: Seed Time and Harvest

In the second day, God created the expanse that would contain His creation. He then established boundaries and division between the waters above and the waters beneath. Observing what He has wrought, He then called it in order to create a frame of reference that could identify and define it. These are things that had never been done before. They are concepts so fundamental to our understanding, that we don't realize that they in themselves were created by God's hand as a message to you and I. God is conveying truth to us about Himself. He didn't do all this with a wave of His hand. He could have, but He did not. He wants us to know something about Himself in order to identify His handiwork in our lives, that we might cooperate with Him and emulate Him as dear children.

When you are facing difficulty, what is your response? What is to BE your response? The world is immersed in situational ethics and a relativistic viewpoint. In other words, the world says, whatever your response is, that it is validated by the fact that you chose to respond to the challenges of life in the manner that you have. The world says, "to each his own, as long as you don't impinge on the individuality of another". The only way the world can conceive of harmony and peace is to call all of mankind to worship at the altar of individualism. Man is so committed to his individuality that he excludes anything higher than himself, and in so doing, has isolated himself and cast himself into the chains of a world where he has nowhere to turn but to himself for help.

The Christian worldview on the other hand, is that there is a God in heaven who bids us to run in the way of His commandments. In the Old Testament, the commandments were laid out in minute detail. In the New Testament, God takes Jesus – the personification of His law, and causes Him to dwell in our hearts by faith to initiate in our lives a process – a spiritual discipline whereby we cooperate with His process in hopes of seeing an Edenic entitlement restored to us that was lost in the fall.

When you see chaos in your life, as God looked out on the formless deep, what is to be your response?

[Eph 5:1 KJV] 1 Be ye therefore followers of God, as dear children;

We are to do what God did. We are to move by our human spirit upon the face of that deep and to speak as God spoke. He considered the chaos and the darkness that was upon the deep and He spoke the thing desired:

18

"Light be.."

What are you saying about the darkness on the face of your deep (your life)? Are you saying "it sure is dark out there?" Wrong answer! You are to be a follower (imitator) of God. You are not God, but you are to be a follower or imitator of God. You have no power in yourself to back up what happens next, but we are to ridiculously look out upon that which we have no control over and say, "light be!" Guess what happens next? God endorses your will and your words, because He has ratified a covenant with you to do so, in the shed blood of Calvary.

That's all we have to do, right? Just speak it out and that is the end of the matter? Some think this is the teaching of the "word of faith" movement. Just say it and that is all that is necessary. This is the "blab and grab" criticism that in some ways has been justified to the extent that many in the faith movement stopped with saying it, and didn't go on. Saying it is only the beginning of what God did. He first brooded, and moved or "fluttered" over the face of the deep, discerning it and determining what He was going to do. He wasn't speaking blindly. When you speak, if you want your words to have power, you must first move upon the face of the deep, by your human spirit, to discern fully what must happen next in the light of God's promise. Most people presumptuously speak their faith, not discerning the circumstance, but denying it, and that is why they never receive.

Having then moved on the deep and spoken over it, what did God do next? He created a firmament – a boundary for that which He had spoken. Are you willing to acknowledge your boundaries? Do you understand the parameters in which you are exercising the God prerogative in your life? There is a jurisdiction within, which you have the authority to act as God acts. To see everything you say and do be as effective as if God said it and did it. This is the humility we are called to. You might think the key to this is merely to know all things are possible – that there are no boundaries.

However, as important as it is to know that all things are possible, you must also accept that there are boundaries. There is jurisdiction. This is what Paul referred to as his "measure", being an apostle to some, but not to all.

So, God moved, He spoke, He created a firmament, then what? He divided. Jesus came not to bring peace but a sword. Many people in their own households, put up with any depth of depravity, sinfulness and darkness because they don't want to rock the boat with their family or create division. They live in fear of not being able to see their children or grandchildren. They tremble at the consequences of creating a separation between light and darkness, as God did, or between the waters (Spirit) above and the waters (spirit) beneath. Therefore, their lives are a hopeless mixture, and they wonder why they never receive from God. You must have the courage to follow through with God's process, for after the brooding, the speaking, accepting of boundary and jurisdiction, there is then division. When you ask God for an answer, He often doesn't simply dollop a deliverance on your head like whip cream – He rather initiates you into a process that is discernable and learnable, but unfortunately, most people bail out of the answer (process) that God sends when they pray. It is only as we cooperate, that we come then to the next thing after brooding (discerning), speaking, accepting boundary, and enduring division. We THEN come to the CALLING. What then?

9 And God said, Let the waters under the heaven be gathered together unto one place, and let the dry [land] appear: and it was so. 10 And God called the dry [land] Earth; and the gathering together of the waters called he Seas: and God saw that [it was] good. 11 And God said, Let the earth bring forth grass, the herb yielding seed, [and] the fruit tree yielding fruit after his kind, whose seed [is] in itself, upon the earth: and it was so. 12 And the earth brought forth grass, [and] herb yielding seed after his kind, and the tree yielding fruit, whose seed [was] in itself, after his kind: and God saw that [it was] good. 13 And the evening and the morning were the third day.

The most significant thing that happens on the third day is the establishing of seed-time and harvest. Notice however, that the processes and elements of process are ongoing. He is still speaking, still establishing boundaries, still dividing. These aspects of God's process are not intermittent or terminal (having an end of the matter and then moving on). You must have the maturity that once God has spoken, you are to speak and keep speaking. Once God has set your boundaries, you are to continually discern them and seek them out. The apostle Paul did this continually. He was always pressing out into his extremity to know just what his boundaries were:

[Act 16:7 KJV] 7 After they were come to Mysia, they assayed to go into Bithynia: but the Spirit suffered them not.

Are you looking for an opportunity to just see a manifestation of God's promise, and then sit down till Jesus comes? You are falling short of your calling. Do you see that you must cooperate with God's process – His ongoing process to move in maturity through the acceptance of the discipleship of the Spirit? We must be willing to experience and install in our character the aspects of God's person and personality, by which we face every day:

1. Moving (brooding)
2. Speaking
3. Setting and Accepting Boundaries
4. Dividing (standing up for something)

In order that we might come to the calling of God. People ask, "what is My calling", and that is a good question. Until you experience the calling of God, you will never be a Lord of your own harvest. You will never come into the THIRD DAY of God where the law of sowing and reaping is established, not only in the earth, but IN YOUR EARTH. Many people try to give and sacrifice, and take advantage of the law of seed time and harvest, and they wonder why it isn't working? It is because they are trying to circumvent God's process. The law of sowing and reaping is a THIRD DAY dynamic that you cannot see established in your life as God intends, until you become accountable to what PRECEEDS THIS.

The third day concept is very prominent in scripture, although many don't understand it. They sing songs about the third day, they name musical groups after the third day, but has anyone ever explored and sought out what the third day is as a part of God's process in our lives? The third day is where the seeds of your obedience produce the fruit of your destiny. Why can't we do this right out of the gate? Because the processes of God that precede seed time and harvest in the seven days of God's process, are intended to extract from the ground of our lives all of those things that we DON'T want to come to seed, fruit and harvest in our experience.

The third day was established in the Old Testament as a day of expectation. It is a day when things that have preceded before are coming to fruition (seed time and harvest):

> *[Exo 19:15- KJV] 15 And he said unto the people, Be ready against the third day: come not at [your] wives.*

The third day was experienced by the Israelites in the wilderness, and a day that God responded to their obedience to gather to Him around the mount of Moses:

> *[Exodus 19:16 – KJV] And it came to pass on the third day in the morning, that there were thunders and lightnings, and a thick*

cloud upon the mount, and the voice of the trumpet exceeding loud;
so that all the people that [was] in the camp trembled.

The third day was a day of full consumption of all that God has for us, and the full measure of the sacrifice of our lives to His service:

[Lev 7:17 KJV] 17 But the remainder of the flesh of the sacrifice on the third day shall be burnt with fire.

Prophetically, the third day is the third 1000-year period after the resurrection of Jesus that predicts the return of Christ and the establishing of His rule upon the earth (1000-year reign).

[Hos 6:2 KJV] 2 After two days will he revive us: in the third day he will raise us up, and we shall live in his sight.

The third day was the day that Jesus predicted that His body, planted in seed time and harvest, would be resurrected in glory:

[Mat 16:21 KJV] 21 From that time forth began Jesus to shew unto his disciples, how that he must go unto Jerusalem, and suffer many things of the elders and chief priests and scribes, and be killed, and be raised again the third day.

These truths are presented in scripture at the macro or cosmic level of creation and in the life of Jesus our Lord. They are nonetheless true guide stones by which God acts in our life. Can you identify what day you are in – in God's process? Are you in the first day, looking at nothing but chaos and darkness? Then you know what to do – SPEAK! Are you in the second day of needing to know just what your boundaries are (what the boundaries of your PERSONAL FIRMAMENT are?). Then you should commit yourself to finding that out as Paul did. What is your measure?

Are you willing to humble yourself to God's mandate in your life, that though others may, you cannot? Are you hesitant to allow the sword to establish division in your life between light and darkness? Then you are stuck in the second day. You want third day reaping and harvest, but you aren't going to get there until you deal with what comes first.

In the third day, you not only experience the harvest, but you become Lord over your harvest. In the third day, God didn't just observe seed time and harvest – He initiated it. How could He do that? Because He was a law to Himself, higher than the law of seed time and harvest. If you are ever going to see the law of sowing and reaping work for you, beyond just being an observer, you must be willing to rise above that law and lord over it as God did with His words and what He did before initiating seed time and harvest, to assure that what happened was according to His will. You can become a LORD over your OWN HARVEST. You can INVOKE the Amos 9:13 dynamic and see the seeds you sow produce a harvest before they hit the ground. You can see the consistent cycle of seed-fruit-harvest as a continual benefit, maintaining and sustaining your life without diminishment – as you fulfill the days of God, giving Him the cooperation He is asking for and maturing into the full measure of the third day dynamic of heaven in your life and your person.

CHAPTER 4

DAY FOUR

Review:

The Genesis account is instructional for us in a devotional way because 1 Cor. 10:11 tells us that the Old Testament narrative is given as an example and instruction for us spiritually, upon whom the ends of the earth are come:

> *[1Co 10:11 KJV] 11 Now all these things happened unto them for ensamples: and they are written for our admonition, upon whom the ends of the world are come.*

After over 100 years of building the ark, God told Noah in Gen. 7:4, that in seven days He would cause it to rain.

> *[Gen 7:4 KJV] 4 For yet seven days, and I will cause it to rain upon the earth forty days and forty nights; and every living substance that I have made will I destroy from off the face of the earth.*

This is always God's answer to "how long oh, Lord?" and "what time is it?" Peter declares to us in 2 Pe. 3:8, that a day with the Lord is as a thousand years and a thousand years is as a day. That tells us that we are moving into the seventh 1000 year day from creation. That eschatologically predicts the advent of the millennial reign of Christ upon the earth.

The word "create" appears seven times in the creation account of Gen. 1 and 2. It speaks of God's process. He chose to create in seven days, instead of an instantaneous creation, in order to say something to us of His divine, anointed process. There are seven days in God's process as He moves you to His Sabbath rest.

[Heb 4:11 KJV] 11 Let us labour therefore to enter into that rest, lest any man fall after the same example of unbelief.

Hebrews 4:11 tells us to labor to enter into the rest of God. Do we have an example of laboring to enter into rest? The very first account of creation of the earth is described as six days in which God labored and a seventh day in which He rested. When you labor, you do not do so in some random way of your own choice. Laboring implies following the instructions of a Master. In the six days of creation then, we see the labors that bring us to rest. All else is just vain religious striving.

Day One:

God moved on the face of the deep and ...

God spoke that which He desired. So, we should move on the face of our deep (our potential) and speak (verbalize) the things that we desire.

Day Two:

God established boundaries for His creation (firmament). We should find out our boundaries, as Paul spoke of ministering within His measure and spiritual jurisdiction (2 Cor. 10:13).

God divided the waters (Spirit) above from the waters (spirit) beneath. We must not live in mixture of the carnal and the spiritual. Jesus didn't come to bring peace, but a sword (Matt. 10:34).

God called. He had never done this before. What God creates, He calls. We must cooperate with His processes prior to this, or calling doesn't come.

Day Three:

Seedtime and harvest are established. This is where you become Lord over your own harvest – but it doesn't happen until you walk through what comes previous to this (moving on the face of your deep by the Spirit, speaking the thing desired, accepting and establishing boundaries in your life and dealing with mixture at the cost of division, if necessary, in your natural lives). The call that comes is the call to step into the Third Day Dynamic of Seed Time and Harvest. This is the Amos 9:13 Entitlement of every believer, who walk themselves into the Third Day experience of the Plowman Overtaking the Reaper.

[Amo 9:13 KJV] 13 Behold, the days come, saith the LORD, that the plowman shall overtake the reaper, and the treader of grapes him that soweth seed; and the mountains shall drop sweet wine, and all the hills shall melt.

We have covered day one of creation through day three. Now let us consider the fourth day of God's process:

[Gen 1:14-19 KJV] 14 And God said, Let there be lights in the firmament of the heaven to divide the day from the night; and let them be for signs, and for seasons, and for days, and years: 15 And let them be for lights in the firmament of the heaven to give light upon the earth: and it was so. 16 And God made two great lights; the greater light to rule the day, and the lesser light to rule the night: [he made] the stars also. 17 And God set them in the firmament of the heaven to give light upon the earth, 18 And to rule over the day and over the night, and to divide the light from the darkness: and God saw that [it was] good. 19 And the evening and the morning were the fourth day.

Now we see the celestial bodies created to contain and reflect the light that God created on the first day. Here we see that God never plants anything in a row. He made light first, and the sun, moon and stars second. If we already had light, what did we need these luminary bodies for? Verse 14 tells us that these bodies are utilized to channel light, to further divide the day from the night, and to be for signs and for seasons. When the day and night are divided then, you can tell the difference, spiritually speaking, and know what your assignment is. You may ask "what are you talking about..?" I'm talking about how Jesus thought in His earth walk:

[Jhn 9:4 KJV] 4 I must work the works of him that sent me, while it is day: the night cometh, when no man can work.

There is a time to work and a time to do something else. If you can't work at night, what can you do (actively speaking)? During the day, you see what is in front of you. At night, you see what is taking place in the heavens. During the day, the sun, which represents God in our lives, is shining so brightly that we can only deal with what He is illuminating for us. Have you ever been in that place where God was working mightily in your life and people came around trying to get you distracted? They want you to look at this problem or that problem, but you don't have time. You are like Nehemiah when Sanballat wanted to distract him from doing what God told him to do:

[Neh 6:3 KJV] 3 And I sent messengers unto them, saying, I [am] doing a great work, so that I cannot come down: why should the work cease, whilst I leave it, and come down to you?

This is what Jesus is referring to when He said "work while it is day..." What is the work? John 5:19 tells us the work that Jesus stayed occupied with:

[Jhn 5:19 KJV] 19 Then answered Jesus and said unto them, Verily, verily, I say unto you, The Son can do nothing of himself, but what he seeth the Father do: for what things soever he doeth, these also doeth the Son likewise.

In the day, you are focused on what is right in front of you and occupying yourself with the Father's business. Now when it is night – that is the time when God opens your eyes to see in the heavens, what is going on behind the curtain of the natural. What are you looking at? People. That is what the sun, moon and stars represent. In Gen. 37:9, Joseph dreamed that he saw his parents and his brethren like the sun, moon and stars making obeisance to him. In Genesis 15, God told Abraham to look at the stars and then clarified for him that what he was really looking at was his seed – his sons and daughters to come.

[Gen 15:5 KJV] 5 And he brought him forth abroad, and said, Look now toward heaven, and tell the stars, if thou be able to number them: and he said unto him, So shall thy seed be.

When God told Abraham to TELL the stars, the word he used was "stele", which is an ancient writing instrument. He wasn't just telling Abraham to count, He was telling Abraham to connect the dots. God promised that Abraham's seed would be as the stars of the heavens, the sand of the seas and the dust of the earth. Abraham had three sets of children:

Ishmael – the Sand Seed (Gen. 17:20).

Isaac – the Star Seed (Gen. 15:5).

Sons of Keturah – Dust Seed (Gen. 25:6).

Stars are set in constellations, whose origin dates back to the Hebrew Mazzaroth:

[Job 38:32 KJV] 32 Canst thou bring forth Mazzaroth in his season? or canst thou guide Arcturus with his sons?

This is the Hebrew "Zodiac" that pre-dated the Greek system. The Mazzaroth was established by God, whereby the heavens (you and I) declare the glory of God:

[Psa 19:1 KJV] 1 [[To the chief Musician, A Psalm of David.]] The heavens declare the glory of God; and the firmament sheweth his handywork.

Have you ever wondered how you wound up in the unusual relationships you have with other Christians? As a believer, you have fellowship and relationship with people whose only connection or commonality to you is found in Christ. They are in your constellation. Constellations were created originally by God to declare the gospel. God placed you in the society of believers you are in, not randomly, but because He is saying something to the world and to you about those relationships if you have the discernment to "tell the stars".

Now – not everyone in your life is a star. Some people in your lives are just big, hot balls of gas. You know who I am speaking of. Faces just flashed before your eyes when you read this. This is where discernment comes in. When you come to a place in God that you have moved on the face of your deep, and spoke creatively in concert with God's blessing for your life, people will be attracted to you. When you accept the boundaries, and set the boundaries that God lays out for you, and make the division that causes mixture to dissipate, it will attract people to your life that will require discernment. When you move into God's third day, where you become Lord of your own harvest and everything you say and do becomes as effective as if God said it or did it – people are going to seek you out.

Have you ever seen someone come into a sum of money? They were broke once and had very few friends. Then things changed and suddenly they are surrounded by every second cousin, family friend and buddy. This is a time that discernment needs to take place. When you need to look past the surface and say of the people around you, are they "dust seed", "sand seed" or "star seed"? What am I talking about? I'm glad you asked.

Planets. What are planets? They are big balls of dust. Dust is the serpent's food (Gen. 3:14). They don't produce light (God is light), they only absorb light and to some degree, reflect light. We identify the planets orbiting ancient stars by the light they reflect. You identify people in your life by the light they reflect. Do you see God reflecting off of them, or something else? Remember that Abraham knew what he was dealing with where the sons of Keturah were concerned. He gave them gifts and sent them away. Do you ever have people give you a prayer request but you know they are after something else? These are the dust seed relationships in your life.

31

If you are the star seed of God (and you are), there are going to be people in orbit around you that are like planets. They will benefit by being in your life but there is no life, no glory and little benefit to be had from them. The sun does not benefit from the earth, the earth benefits from the sun. You need to know the difference, otherwise, you will put expectations on the dust seed relationships in your life and get offended and off track with what God is doing in your life.

Let's look at another metaphor of planetary bodies to identify relational dangers you will experience as you find your place in one of God's constellations of relationship:

[Jde 1:12-13 KJV] 12 These are spots in your feasts of charity, when they feast with you, feeding themselves without fear: clouds [they are] without water, carried about of winds; trees whose fruit withereth, without fruit, twice dead, plucked up by the roots; 13 Raging waves of the sea, foaming out their own shame; wandering stars, to whom is reserved the blackness of darkness for ever.

What is a wandering star? It really isn't a star, but a comet. A comet is similar in make up to a planet with one exception – it has no stable orbit and its composition is dominated by ice. Watch out for the people who blaze across the scene in your life and your church. They make a big splash and call attention to themselves, but there is ice water in their veins. They are very compelling. People think comets are spiritual events. They think comets are prophetic. But all they do is make a scene and draw attention to themselves and then they are gone once again into the darkness from which they came. You need to identify these people and save yourself from meddling with them. No matter how spiritual they may seem – withdraw from them. Do not let your orbit transect the trajectory of their agenda, or you may have a planetary disaster that you will have to clean up.

God made planets, stars and comets after making light itself, because in the human condition there is very little unified consistency. Different stars cast a different light. Some bodies (or people) cast no light at all, but they will be in your personal orbit most, if not all of your life. You have to know who they are and you have to know who you are. When you begin to walk in the edenic entitlement of God's third day – the very next and most important lesson you need to learn is to read the signs and seasons, and look past the natural into the heavens, so you know what is going on and what is coming next.

CHAPTER 5

DAY FIVE

Be Fruitful and Multiply:

> *Gen. 1:20 And God said, Let the waters bring forth abundantly the moving creature that hath life, and fowl [that] may fly above the earth in the open firmament of heaven. 21 And God created great whales, and every living creature that moveth, which the waters brought forth abundantly, after their kind, and every winged fowl after his kind: and God saw that [it was] good. 22 And God blessed them, saying, Be fruitful, and multiply, and fill the waters in the seas, and let fowl multiply in the earth. 23 And the evening and the morning were the fifth day.*

We now come to the fifth day of God's process. Again, as we study the events of day five of creation, we are reminded that God never does anything random or without impart to you and I. Wisdom and understanding, not only regarding what God has done, but what He is doing and will do in our lives if we cooperate with His purposes. The things that take place on the fifth day are not independent of what has passed on before. We see God creating fish and fowl and we realize that since water above and beneath the firmament existed on the second day, that He could have added these creatures to the earth then, but did not. This is all about what has to happen in our lives before the blessing of verse 22, "be fruitful and multiply" can be pronounced over our lives.

Remember that the study of God's process is an inquiry, the end of which will answer the questions for us, "how long oh God?" and "what time is it?" We cannot step into being fruitful and multiplying without cooperating with what is revealed of God's process that precedes the sixth day. God is giving us a template and a pattern for cooperating with His creative process that is ongoing in our lives, even at the most personal and subjective level. He will not act, for instance, to bring about fifth day blessing until we have accepted second day responsibility. What do I mean by this? Let us review:

1. Day One – identify your potential (deep) and the darkness that is encroaching upon it (upon your life). Then do in your life what God did in the beginning: SPEAK with specificity over your unrealized potential the thing that you desire (light be). It is important that we actually verbalize this. Prayer that is not verbalized is often only wishful thinking. Be verbal and out loud in speaking over the darkness that is encroaching the deeps of your potential in God.

2. Day Two - Accept your boundaries. Know that over every life, there is a measure or jurisdiction that God sets. You must inquire after this and accept it as the yoke easy and burden light responsibility in your life. I once had a dear friend who moved in an astonishingly accurate and powerful prophetic word. Yet late one night, he disclosed to me that in his view, he had no boundaries or limitations in life or in God. That man is in prison today for the remainder of

his natural life. He refused to accept boundaries. He never came to grips with day two in God.

You also must deal with mixture. The waters of the Spirit above (God's spirit) and the waters below (man's spirit) must be discerned. You have to know the difference. You must rightly divide, for the things you speak out of the Day One dynamic, will come to pass rightly or wrongly, and you don't want, by failure to discern, to bring disaster upon your life or the lives of others. This is not a one-time affair. It is an ongoing discipline. Deal unceasingly with mixture in your life.

Having spoken over your deep, accepted boundary and limitation and dealt with mixture – NOW God calls. Now you are ready to be called into the third day responsibility that comes with the law of Seedtime and Harvest being installed in your life.

3. Day Three – Seed time and harvest. Now you are ready to become Lord of your own harvest. Until mixture and innate rebellion are dealt with (Day Two), it would be a curse to allow your life to produce what is in the soil of your heart. Now that the disciplines of spirit revealed in Day One and Day Two of God's process are installed in your life, you can do what Hebrews 6:1 speaks of and "go on" in God to see the law of harvest actually begin to work effectively in your life:

> *[Heb 6:1 NKJV] 1 Therefore, leaving the discussion of the elementary [principles] of Christ, let us go on to perfection, not laying again the foundation of repentance from dead works and of faith toward God,*

4. Day Four – when you come into Third Day blessing and benefit in your life, you are going to gain a reputation for getting your prayers answered. This is a dangerous time to be without

discernment. The curtain of the heavens must be drawn back and you need to be able to identify the relationships that will suddenly become abundant around you. It has been said that a man who is poor is a man who has few friends. A man who is wealthy has many friends, but none that he can be sure of. This is not the whole truth, but it is a truism.

In Day Four, we see the celestial bodies created that represents various relationships in our lives. Joseph dreamed of his parents and brothers as the sun, moon and stars. God told Abraham his children would be as the stars of the heavens. Jude warns about those in our midst who were merely wandering stars – twice dead, trees plucked up, waves foaming out their shame. When blessing and prosperity begin to come, as in the Third Day time of seed time and harvest, we need the discernment of looking through the natural perspective and the appearance of things, to know who and what we are actually dealing with.

Day Five: Be Fruitful and Multiply
Why do we have to wait so long before blessing comes? I thought I was ready to pastor a church of a 1000 people when I was 21. Why would I have to wait? Jesus warned His own family members about their poor sense of spiritual timing:

[Jhn 7:6 KJV] 6 Then Jesus said unto them, My time is not yet come: but your time is alway ready.

Regardless of your station in life, if you follow after God, sooner or later you will step into a place of blessing, prosperity and privilege. It is God's base nature to go first class all the way. It takes much false doctrine and error to brutalize God's people with poverty, want and deprivation. The church has worked very hard at this through the centuries, even establishing in the Middle Ages a "vow of poverty" that deeply contaminates Christian thinking today. Christians rejoice and get downright giddy when their favorite sports figure earns obscene amounts of money for swinging a stick at a ball, but their offense knows no bounds when their pastor gets a new car or enjoys a financial status above the poverty line. What are these people (and there are many) going to do when they answer to God for their religious attitudes about money and blessing, when they stand before a God whose city gates are of pearl, with streets of gold, and God on a throne of emerald and precious jewels? This is one of the deepest and most fundamental needs of repentance in the church still today, as any minister or pastor worth his salt can readily agree.

There is a place in the outlying of God's process in your life that you will begin to be fruitful and multiply. Blessing will not be simply the occasional good things that punctuate a life of struggle and difficulty. Blessing will be your base state – the default nature of your experience in God and the result manifesting prosperity and benefit in your personal life. This is the inevitable outcome of all that pursue hot after God, unless they have worked very hard to talk themselves out of the dividends of the cross. Fruitfulness will come. It will not be the mere adding of good things, but the exponential multiplying of the good things of God across the full spectrum of your life.

This "being fruitful and multiplying" comes because you have complied and accepted the discipline of God's process, and now God says it is time. Blessing will now, not be an intermittent thing, but rather the intrinsic nature of the ongoing and upward trajectory of your life. With this will come influence, position and conspicuous testimony. There is a responsibility that comes with the blessing of God. People are watching you. People are depending on you. There are people that won't make it in life, or in God, without the example that you are called now to demonstrate. If you falter or fail, your life will not be the only one made ship wreck.

This is why God withholds the "be fruitful and multiplying" until other disciplines that must come first, are established in your life. If you haven't accepted boundary and limitation, being fruitful and multiplying will ultimately not be a blessing in your life. You will take the blessing of God, as Solomon unfortunately did, and squander it on dissipation and personal idolatry. Your life, as Solomon's, will become more of a cautionary tale, rather than a glorious example of the goodness of God in the land of the living.

If you were to be fruitful and multiply before you discerned the potential of your deep, and dispelled by the word of faith the darkness encroaching on your life, then when the fruitfulness came, the darkness would increase along with everything else. You would become a spiritual pariah – blessed and multiplying, but no one can stand to be around you because you didn't deal with your own personal darkness and didn't deal with the mixture in your life. It is God's grace that He withholds the "be fruitful and multiply" benediction over your life. Solomon, at long last, understood this principle when resigning himself to the reality of being a vessel of lesser honor in the house of God, he observed:

[Pro 10:22 KJV] 22 The blessing of the LORD, it maketh rich, and he addeth no sorrow with it.

Solomon took the blessing of God, intended for his good, and re-scinded the fidelity of his youth for the lust of the flesh, and paid for it with a tainted testimony that has stained his reputation for 1000's of years. Do not be this person. You should at this point in our study, come to the place that you are not just being informed, but being convicted. Where are you in God's process? Have you discerned the darkness moving on the face of your deep, or are you living in denial? Have you declared what God says about your situation, or are you just rehashing the negative? Are you now willing to accept God's mandate of boundary and limitations in very intimate areas of potential and outright personal idolatry? Are you now ready to deal with mixture in yourself and in your home life? Are you willing to accept the sword that Jesus said He came to bring, even in the most blissful domestic setting of your own personal life?

God is calling you. He is calling you to THIRD DAY lordship over the harvest of God in your life. He is calling you to the place where the plowman overtakes the reaper. He is calling you to open your eyes and discern the character of the lives around you, that you might avoid the wandering stars and the big hot balls of gas – people who are part of the problem and not part of the solution, no matter how spiritual they may seem on the surface. Once you have navigated spiritually into full possession of the law of seedtime and harvest, you become like Solomon. The blessing is there, but what are you ultimately going to do with it? The outworking of the law of seedtime and harvest in your life will result in being fruitful and multiplying. In all of this, God knew even on the fifth day, what was coming in the fall of man. But by this time the die was cast. Are you willing to walk in this place with God? Or are you going to turn back and just be a playpen Christian till Jesus comes?

CHAPTER 6

DAY SIX

Moving into Authority:

In this series of teachings, we are postulating that God not only moves in and by sovereign, independent crisis experiences (one-time events requiring little preparation), He also moves in our lives through deliberative spiritual process that can be learned and applied in every believer's life. This is why Jesus told the Pharisees in Luke 17:20-21, that the kingdom doesn't come by observation. While God does at times sovereignly move with little more than a plaintive cry for help – it is a fact that participation and action on your part is often necessary.

If we are going to be led to understand that faith without works is dead (James 2:17), then we must also inquire of the scriptures by what methodology we might glean understanding of not only how to live in the Spirit, but also to walk (progress by steps) in the Spirit (Gal. 5:25). There is no better starting place then Genesis to begin to uncover, by revelatory inquiry, God's creative process. Through God's seven days, we labor to enter into rest through an understanding of God's process that is comprehensible, reproducible and applicable in every circumstance of our lives.

Looking at Genesis 1:1 – 2:3 as the template of God's process in our lives, by which we must cooperate with His purposes, let us briefly review the days of His creative process in our lives:

1. God moves and speaks. We must move upon the darkness encroaching our deep (potential) and speak as God speaks (Eph. 5:1).
2. God sets a boundary for the heavens (firmament) and divides the water from the waters, and calls these things by a determinate call. Likewise we must discern our boundaries, accept division that removes spiritual mixture in our lives (waters-Spirit above from the waters-spirit beneath). In that arrangement we are prepared to receive the call of God.
3. Having accepted boundary and dealt with mixture in our lives, we receive the call and step into the mastery of the Law of Seedtime and Harvest. The Amos 9:13 reality becomes the dynamic truth of our lives.
4. God creates the luminary bodies of heaven for signs and seasons. When we by faith become Lords of our own harvest, we must be alert to what is happening in the heavenly. We must discern the character (star-seed; sand-seed; dust-seed) regarding the people that will rush around us because we are manifesting the blessing and favor of God, due to willingly collaborating thus far with His purposes revealed in the seven days of His process (see chapter 4).
5. God commands His creation to bring forth abundantly, to multiply and fill the earth – our boundary for creation that He has set. When you have moved upon your darkness and spoken the word; when you have accepted boundary and dealt with mixture. When you have become lord of your own seed-time and harvest and gained discernment by looking into the heavenly realm to understand things around you – THEN you are positioned for full reward. Then life

and life more abundantly are yours by default because you have collaborated and cooperated with the mind of God concerning your circumstance, situation and maturity in the kingdom.

Entering Into Full Authority:

Gen. 1:26 And God said, Let us make man in our image, after our likeness: and let them have dominion over the fish of the sea, and over the fowl of the air, and over the cattle, and over all the earth, and over every creeping thing that creepeth upon the earth. 27 So God created man in his [own] image, in the image of God created he him; male and female created he them. 28 And God blessed them, and God said unto them, Be fruitful, and multiply, and replenish the earth, and subdue it: and have dominion over the fish of the sea, and over the fowl of the air, and over every living thing that moveth upon the earth.…31 And God saw every thing that he had made, and, behold, [it was] very good. And the evening and the morning were the sixth day.

After six days of moving, speaking, creating, dividing and populating the environment of the earth, we find the apex of God's process, when He not only made man, but He gave Him dominion to replenish and to subdue the environment God placed man in. This is the point in God's process, where the responsibility becomes ours regarding all that happens in the setting that God has provided us to live out our lives in.

There is much confusion in this area that has caused men to see themselves as being at the mercy of a capricious God, regarding circumstances or situations that they have no control over. Beyond that, men over the centuries have so misunderstood the hand of God in the earth, and their role in cooperating with God in His process, that they would rather conclude that there is no

God, than accept the responsibility that is man's, to subdue, have dominion and replenish according to the Father's divine plan.

In other words, are we waiting on God – or is God waiting on us? The complaint often comes in the form of the skeptic's questions:

Why do little babies die if God is a loving, all powerful benefactor?

If God exists, why does He allow wars, or tolerate man's inhumanity to man?

Why does sickness, cancer and all manner of suffering plague the hapless victims of such diseases if in fact, as God's word declares, that He will heal, deliver and bless us?

Is God an absentee landlord?

Is God a dead-beat dad who has abandoned us to a creation run amok?

Why does God not act?

Sometimes we come up with the wrong answers because we are not asking the right questions. Theologians, scholars and church leaders have shown themselves far too timid to challenge the validity of the question, yet have concocted libraries full of doctrine and devotional studies that explain that this is all part of God's immutable purpose, that we simply need to realize that we will "understand it better bye and bye" and then go on to define faith as not asking these questions to begin with. This is unmitigated cowardice and completely unnecessary, for God's word addresses these matters in a very thorough manner.

[2Co 1:19-20 KJV] 19 For the Son of God, Jesus Christ, who was preached among you by us, [even] by me and Silvanus and Timotheus, was not yea and nay, but in him was yea. 20 For all the promises of God in him [are] yea, and in him Amen, unto the glory of God by us.

In addressing these matters, Paul teaches in 2 Cor. 1, that a believer cannot possibly be established in His faith until He realizes that God's default answer to every demand upon His promises is yes. Another way of making this statement is:

God will never say no to what the cross says yes to when the conditions of faith, on man's part, are met. In the beginning before the fall, God simply gave man dominion, however, because of the disobedience of Adam, we must look to the cross and the shed blood of Christ to mitigate the disqualification of sin and thereby, through faith, take again the authority and dominion that is inherently ours as new creations in Christ Jesus.

Now who is in charge? Is God in charge, or man, or the devil? That depends on who you ask and on what side of the blood line you are standing. Three times in the gospel of John, Jesus referred to Satan as the prince of this world (John 12:31; John 14:30; John 16:11). Ask yourself the question, did Satan become the god of this world legitimately? If you believe in the teaching that Satan is a fallen angel who successfully fomented rebellion against God's throne before creation, then you would be postulating that Satan became god of this world because of his own disobedience and God's forbearance in dealing with him up to now.

What about man's disobedience? Is this all the devil's fault? Are we acquitted by simply declaring, as the comedian Flip Wilson in the 60's, who famously said "The Devil made me do it?" What about considering the role man's disobedience in the garden had

45

in opening the door for Satan to become the god of this world, the prince of the power of the air? In Gen. 1:28, we find that God gave man authority to subdue and have dominion over all creation. There are no caveats cited or exceptions noted to take into consideration his forbearance (purportedly) in allowing Satan to maintain rule because of prior events in a supposed epoch of precreation, when Satan usurped God's throne in the visible creation. When then might Satan, in this view, have become the prince of the power of the air? At a point when he disobeyed or when man disobeyed? Did God, in His sovereignty, open the door to the enemy, or did man's disobedience open the door to the enemy? Most people never think this deeply on the matter of Satan our enemy, or original sin. We simply have a corpus of traditional doctrine about it and never question or inquire as the Bereans in Acts, to see if these things be so.

You see, the authority that Adam abdicated by disobedience in the garden of Eden, Jesus reclaimed in the garden of Gethsemane. Jesus came as the only begotten of the Father, to become the First Born from the Dead that He might include the race of fallen man as the LAST ADAM and the SECOND MAN of a NEW CREATION that each one of us in Christ are partakers of.

[1Co 15:45 KJV] 45 And so it is written, The first man Adam was made a living soul; the last Adam [was made] a quickening spirit.

When Adam disobeyed, Satan gained the title deed (as it were) to all that was originally man's by the divine decrees of God in Gen. 1:28. At that moment, Satan, by divine right (due to man's disobedience), had the authority to impress upon man HIS image and HIS distorted, perverted nature. If this is true, then why don't we all look like angels? If Satan is an angel, in the manner in which he has been traditionally considered to be so, then why does not man in the depths of sin, display the nature of angels? Instead, man in sin becomes a brute beast, so despicable that even pigs will commit self-destruction (Matt. 8:32) if they are possessed of the nature that is inherent in man's fallen nature, outside of Christ.

In the study of the scriptures, the hermeneutical principles of learned church men maintain that there is a "Law of First Mention" that governs interpretation of various subjects in the study of the scriptures. It reads thusly:

> *The Law of First Mention is "The principle that requires one to go to that portion of the Scriptures where a doctrine is mentioned for the first time and to study the first occurrence of the same in order to get the fundamental inherent meaning of that doctrine."*

Ask yourself – where is Satan first mentioned and what can we learn about him from that reference? If the law of first mention is of any value to us, or holds any validity, then the first mention of Satan must provide us with the fundamental, inherent meaning of who he is.

> *[Gen 3:1 KJV] 1 Now the serpent was more subtil than any beast of the field which the LORD God had made. And he said unto the woman, Yea, hath God said, Ye shall not eat of every tree of the garden?*

What does this verse tell us? Our purpose here is not to do an exhaustive inquiry into the nature of Satan, but looking at this one verse, and weighing it with the universally accepted import conferred upon it by the law of first mention, what can we learn of him? The most emphatic and evident thing we can surmise is that, from the standpoint of holy writ and this book of first things, that Satan originates not in the order of angels, but in the animal kingdom. He is spoken of as "more subtle than any beast of the field..." This does bear out some continuity in comparing the nature of sin as being that of a brute beast in many scriptures throughout the bible.

What about the "fallen angel" theory (not to suggest there are not fallen angels as the bible confirms there are)? Ask yourself the question – if you were the devil, would you like to be thought of as a fallen angel who successfully rebelled against the throne of God, and not only that, but maintained that rebellion for 6000 years? Which glorifies the enemy more? Seeing him as an anointed cherub, the darling of pre-creation – or as Gen. 3:1 plainly tells us, an errant inmate of the order of created beasts that originally were intended to be completely under the dominion of man, by conference of authority by God Himself to man in Gen. 1:28?

> *[1Co 15:47 KJV] 47 The first man [is] of the earth, earthy: the second man [is] the Lord from heaven.*

Paul in the verse above, identifies Jesus in the work of the cross as the progenitor of a new creation. What is true of the Lord is true of those that are his. John declares in his first epistle:

> *[1Jo 4:17 KJV] 17 … as he is, so are we in this world.*

How is He? He is seated at the right hand of the Father. What does this have to do with us? 1 Cor. 12:27 tells us that He is the head and we are His body. What is true of the head is true of the members of the body attached to that head, other than headship itself. If He is Lord then there is lordship in you.

> *[Rev 1:6 KJV] 6 And hath made us kings and priests unto God and his Father; to him [be] glory and dominion for ever and ever. Amen.*

> *[Rev 5:10 KJV] 10 And hast made us unto our God kings and priests: and we shall reign on the earth.*

If Jesus is King of Kings, then we, as members of His body are kings, and this is confirmed in the New Testament by both Peter and John the revelator. What are we saying? What Adam perpetrated by transgression in the garden of Eden, Jesus remediated by obedience in the garden of Gethsemane. He went from the cross and down in to hell and took the keys of death, hell and the grave. When He came out of the grave, whatever authority Satan had, by whatever pretext he had, it was completely undone by Jesus. We might say "well – that is Jesus", but in Christ's own declaration, this wrenching of power away from the enemy has a direct and profound impact upon you:

> *[Mat 28:18-20 KJV] 18 And Jesus came and spake unto them, saying, All power is given unto me in heaven and in earth. 19 Go ye therefore, and teach all nations, baptizing them in the name of the Father, and of the Son, and of the Holy Ghost: 20 Teaching them to observe all things whatsoever I have commanded you: and, lo, I am with you alway, [even] unto the end of the world. Amen.*

The power that is Christ's is ours by divine right as members of the body of Christ. Satan is not the legitimate prince of the power of the air of your life – YOU ARE. You are the principality and the power, and in fact you are, says John the revelator, a king in the earth. Ruling and reigning does not begin after death, it is your portion now. What does that look like? If we are kings and priests, how come we are so powerless? Because we have lived out of a religious philosophy that the Pharisees were guilty of.

> *[Luk 17:20-21 KJV] 20 And when he was demanded of the Pharisees, when the kingdom of God should come, he answered them and said, The kingdom of God cometh not with observation: 21 Neither shall they say, Lo here! or, lo there! for, behold, the kingdom of God is within you.*

These men understood they were powerless, and therefore were looking for something outward and something in the future. This is the perspective of fallen man because he knows just how powerless he is and how bleak his prospects are. Jesus corrects them and says, that the kingdom is not something outward we are hopefully observing will come as an event or outward experience, but rather something inward that must be related to and released by faith, because the kingdom, the deliverance, the healing, the provision, everything that is in the kingdom is in you. The challenge is to come to Him, not only as Savior, but as Lord – submitting to His anointed process, that after 5 days of capitulation and cooperation on our part, we are now ready to stand forth and receive, not only the occasional anointing of an intermittent blessing, but the office and authority that causes everything you say and do to become consistently, throughout life the baseline of your experience.

The sixth day is graduation day out of the process of discipline of God and into the experience of the finished work of Calvary, coming into the chain of custody of your life, from the cross, to the throne, to your inner man crowned with glory and virtue – manifesting His grace, and power and beneficence in your behalf and in behalf of all those round about you.

CHAPTER 7

DAY SEVEN

Arriving at God's Rest:

Now we come to the seventh day of God's process. The seventh day is connected with God's Sabbath Rest.

[Exo 12:16 KJV] 16 And in the first day [there shall be] an holy convocation, and in the seventh day there shall be an holy convocation to you; no manner of work shall be done in them, save [that] which every man must eat, that only may be done of you.

[Exo 20:10 KJV] 10 But the seventh day [is] the sabbath of the LORD thy God: [in it] thou shalt not do any work, thou, nor thy son, nor thy daughter, thy manservant, nor thy maidservant, nor thy cattle, nor thy stranger that [is] within thy gates:

This day connects with the seventh day of the week under the Old Covenant and also the seventh millennia from Adam. According to Hebrew tradition, Adam and Eve were placed in the garden of Eden in the Jewish year 5777. If correct, this chronology would place us within 30 years of the advent of God's seventh millennia from the inception of the world and the placement of mankind in the garden of Eden. This is also tantalizingly synchronous with a third day advent predicted by Hosea:

> [Hos 6:1-3 KJV] 1 Come, and let us return unto the LORD: for he hath torn, and he will heal us; he hath smitten, and he will bind us up. 2 After two days will he revive us: in the third day he will raise us up, and we shall live in his sight. 3 Then shall we know, [if] we follow on to know the LORD: his going forth is prepared as the morning; and he shall come unto us as the rain, as the latter [and] former rain unto the earth.

If, as Peter declared in 2 Peter 3:8, that a thousand years is as a day and a day as a thousand years, then we are equally within approximately 30 years of crossing simultaneously in history the seventh millennia from Adam and the third millennia from the resurrection. It is fascinating that the seventh millennia from Adam and the third millennia from the birth of Christ occur within just a few years of each other and perhaps (due to errors in extant calendar systems used over the centuries) they occur on exactly the same year.

What is to be our personal response to the thought of the eschatological consummation of history? In Luke 9:13 very simply, Jesus commanded, "occupy till I come..." What are we to busy ourselves about? Waiting on a mountain somewhere peering into the sky, anticipating the advent? No, we are to busy ourselves with obeying Matt. 6:33, as the personal mandate for our lives to seek first the kingdom. There is no need to be overly concerned about goods and gold and life's treasures, for all things will be added to us when we seek first the kingdom. This is not simply a general exhortation to be sincere and do our best. There is, discernable in scripture, specific mandates and disciplines of the spirit that are identifiable and practicable by any believer at any point in life. That is the message of this book. As we commit to God's process, we will walk into His outcome and one day that will have a much broader, cataclysmic meaning than we could ever know.

In Hosea 6:1-3, the third day is when "He will raise us up and we will walk in His sight..." and the seventh day, according to Isaiah 2:1-2 when "all the nations shall flow into the mountain of the house of the Lord..." These two points of sacred prognostication, point to one and the same event. This event is not described as some egalitarian, cosmic moment of divine spontaneity, but rather (according to Hosea), something that we walk into, because "then shall we know IF we follow on to know the Lord, that his going forth is prepared as the morning; and He shall come unto us as the rain, as the latter and former rain unto the earth..." The metaphor of rain implies a participatory outpouring of God's spirit, similar, yet greater in magnitude than what we have seen or at least have record of in contemporary or ancient Christian history. In other words – something we are not only WAITING ON but also WALKING INTO.

This has implications for us both eschatologically as the global body of Christ in the earth, and personally as we choose to not only live in the Spirit but also walk in the Spirit (Gal. 5:25) – into the Seventh day of God's rest, the Third day of going on to know Him in the former and latter rain as Joel prophesied "in the first month..." (Joel 2:23).

The Character of God's Rest:

[Gen 2:1-3 KJV] 1 Thus the heavens and the earth were finished, and all the host of them. 2 And on the seventh day God ended his work which he had made; and he rested on the seventh day from all his work which he had made. 3 And God blessed the seventh day, and sanctified it: because that in it he had rested from all his work which God created and made.

Now God rests from His labors. This is what Paul referred to in Hebrews 4:

> *[Heb 4:9-11 KJV] 9 There remaineth therefore a rest to the people of God. 10 For he that is entered into his rest, he also hath ceased from his own works, as God [did] from his. 11 Let us labour therefore to enter into that rest, lest any man fall after the same example of unbelief.*

Now this is not merely going to heaven and sitting on a fleecy white cloud. This is not sitting back in stagnation waiting on God to do something that He has left up to us to be the participants of. The final act of God, where Adam and Eve were concerned, was to confer authority on them, to have dominion and to subdue the earth. When God entered into His rest, having given man (you and I) dominion, there were specific things we were expected to do:

> *[Gen 2:15 KJV] 15 And the LORD God took the man, and put him into the garden of Eden to dress it and to keep it.*

The word used in commanding Adam and Eve to "dress" the garden of Eden includes the meaning of "to compel it to produce" or to "compel to serve for another". Adam, by the authority given him by God, could open his mouth and by the example God set in six days of creation, compel the earth to carry out God's plan. This is the mandate of declaration spoken of in Job:

> *[Job 22:28 KJV] 28 Thou shalt also decree a thing, and it shall be established unto thee: and the light shall shine upon thy ways.*

The word established there means that the thing decreed shall "rise up before thee". After man fell, he lost the ability to exercise this dominion. Therefore God told him in Gen.3:19, that he would have to do the work himself and make his living in the sweat of his face till he returned to the dust from whence he came. What it was intended he should do as the personification of God's image on the earth – now, being outside of Christ in a fallen condition, he must do by the sweat of his brow.

What Adam perpetrated in the fall, bringing man under the curse and losing his God given authority – Jesus in His redemptive act of sacrifice remediated. What Adam lost in the fall through his disobedience, Jesus restores to man by faith in the shed blood of Calvary:

[Rom 5:15-19 KJV] 15 But not as the offence, so also [is] the free gift. For if through the offence of one many be dead, much more the grace of God, and the gift by grace, [which is] by one man, Jesus Christ, hath abounded unto many. 16 And not as [it was] by one that sinned, [so is] the gift: for the judgment [was] by one to condemnation, but the free gift [is] of many offences unto justification. 17 For if by one man's offence death reigned by one; much more they which receive abundance of grace and of the gift of righteousness shall reign in life by one, Jesus Christ.) 18 Therefore as by the offence of one [judgment came] upon all men to condemnation; even so by the righteousness of one [the free gift came] upon all men unto justification of life. 19 For as by one man's disobedience many were made sinners, so by the obedience of one shall many be made righteous.

That word "righteous" not only defines as upright, but also implies "entitled". You are entitled in the cross to be a god-man upon the earth through faith, not in yourself, but in the efficacious work of Christ on the cross.

God's Rest is Not Inactivity:
Realize that the rest in God is not inactivity. It isn't sitting on the porch in your sock feet with a straw in your mouth and the theme

song to "Hee Haw" playing in the background. What God actually did was spin His processes into the earth by His hand and His word, and then infused them with the forward momentum of His eternal power to proceed along the curve of time and eternity until (as the Quantum theorists would agree) creation turns back on itself to consummate God's purposes at the end of the age. This is the day in which you and I live.

As is the cosmic activity of God, so likewise, we find in our infinitesimal lives, a like process at work that is discernable, which we can identify and cooperate with in our own daily lives. What does the rest of God look like at ground level of the everyday believer's experience? You will know it as that season of life where you know that the momentum of blessing and favor begins to carry you out of the reach of the rigors and pitfalls of the fallen environment that you find yourself in.

It will be that moment when you move in your faith from the pressure of failure to the pressure of success. Paul warned the churches of Acts in his first missionary journey of just this eventuality:

> *[Act 14:22 KJV] 22 Confirming the souls of the disciples, [and] exhorting them to continue in the faith, and that we must through much tribulation enter into the kingdom of God.*

That word tribulation is not cancer, accident or catastrophe. It is that time when the momentum of God's blessing in your life becomes as Jesus declared in Luke 6:38;

> *[Luk 6:38 KJV] 38 Give, and it shall be given unto you; good measure, pressed down, and shaken together, and running over, shall men give into your bosom. For with the same measure that ye mete withal it shall be measured to you again.*

The emphasis in Jesus' statement above is PRESSED DOWN, or PRESSURE! This is the pressure that you encounter as you are walking in the kingdom, cooperating with God's word and His ways, insomuch as He reveals them to you on a moment by moment basis. Now your forward momentum is not because you are hanging on to God but because He is carrying you into a whole new metric of favor and blessing, that in reality, is accompanied with a much greater pressure than any failure you have ever faced.

Most people know nothing of the pressure of success at this level. The pressure of success is much greater than the pressure of failure, it just has a different outcome. In fact, the pressure of success is MUCH MORE BRUTAL than the pressure of failure. The pressure of success also has a much more unknowable outcome. We all know where the pressure of failure is taking us: ROCK BOTTOM. That is familiar territory for most people. They know what failure looks like. They are familiar with repossessed cars, late mortgage payments, broken relationships, broken bodies, etc., we all know and are acquainted with heartbreak. The deception is this – that the FLESH, the beast nature in fallen man, will choose the familiar EVERYTIME rather than face the rigors of trusting God for an unknowable outcome, even if it leads to favor, benefit and the dividends of the kingdom being manifest in your life beyond your wildest expectations.

You will have entered into the rest of God when you suddenly realize that all those prayers and faith confessions you made for decades, have suddenly laid hold on your life, and are thrusting you into the harvest of God at an astonishing speed and immense intensity that could pale the courage of the boldest among us. When you realize that the fear of God is not that He will NOT act in your life, but that He WILL, and did you really know what you were asking for when you prayed all those desperate prayers years ago?

If you will commit yourself to God's process, you will see EVERY PRAYER ANSWERED and EVERY PROPHETIC WORD over your life come to pass. I am here to testify as one man whose every prophetic word came to pass in a matter of a few short years when I began to abandon myself to God's deliberative process as testified to in this book. I walked off my personal map onto a blank GPS grid in which I stood in the depth of a field of all possibility, having no clue what God was going to do next, and knowing that His goodness would come upon Me and overtake me, whether I could take it or not, before I could make my next move. This is what life on the cutting edge of God's purposes looks like. It may manifest differently for every person, but this experience has your name written on it, if you will just commit and make a decision that you will no longer be one that is WAITING ON, but rather one that is WALKING INTO, by God's revealed deliberative process, that which has been promised to you.

Made in the USA
San Bernardino, CA
03 June 2017